Contents

Fi...
Running Tracks
page 2

Play
A Beast in the Bushes
page 22

Poem
The Beast
page 28

Non-fiction
A Famous Castaway
page 30

Written by
Lou Kuenzler

Illustrated by
Nelson Evergreen

Series editor **Dee Reid**

Before reading
Running Tracks

Characters

| Lena | Eleven | Tariq | Ricky |

Tricky words

ch1 p3	javelin	ch2 p8	mysteriously
ch1 p3	lotion	ch2 p10	wandered
ch1 p4	swallowed	ch2 p10	shuddered
ch2 p8	serious	ch4 p16	peering

Story starter

Two teams of young athletes were stranded on a desert island after a plane crash. Lena was a javelin thrower with North Athletic. The other team, Sport Squad, divided the island in half and made each team hunt for food on their own side. The Sport Squad athletes were known only by the number on their vests. Number Eleven came to see Lena with a warning.

Running Tracks

Chapter One

The beach was empty. I laid my javelin on the sand and stepped into the sea. I splashed cool water on my arms. My pale skin was burning in the hot sun. If I was on holiday, Mum would have said, "Lena, put on some sun lotion," but this wasn't a holiday. I was stranded on this desert island with my athletics team. Mum was thousands of miles away.

I swallowed hard. I missed home so much it made my stomach hurt. I even missed my little sister, and I used to think she was a pain!

I splashed water on my face. Suddenly, a fish darted between my feet. I could have speared it if I had my javelin in my hand. We needed all the food we could get. I was supposed to be hunting, but I had put the javelin down for a moment. I turned to reach for it, but a voice shouted from the sand dunes.

"Don't move!" it said.
I saw a flash of silver. A javelin splashed into the pool and speared the fish. A tall boy strolled across the sand.
"You've got to admit, that was a good shot!" he grinned.

He was wearing the green running vest of our rival team, the Sport Squad. On his vest was the number eleven.

"What do you think you're doing?" I gasped. "You could have killed me!"

"I could have," said Number Eleven, "but I didn't. I've come to bring your team a warning."

Chapter Two

Number Eleven held up the fish and grinned. He wasn't supposed to be here. This was our land. Sport Squad had divided the island in half. They said each team should keep to their own side and only hunt there. Now Eleven was here, cheating and stealing our food.

Sport Squad would do anything to survive.

"What did you want to warn us about?" I asked.

Eleven looked serious. "There's a killer beast on the island," he said. "Don't go out alone. It's dangerous."

"A beast?" I asked.

"Number Five, who is our youngest hurdler, mysteriously disappeared," said Eleven.

"You mean Rosa – the girl about eight years old with freckles?" I gasped. I remembered her from when we first got on the plane. I had told Rosa she looked like my sister and I offered her a sweet.

The Sport Squad's captain told her not to talk to me and snatched the sweet away. "What do you mean she has disappeared?" I asked. My heart was pounding.

"She wandered away from camp after dark," Eleven said. "All we found in the morning was this …" He held up a small white running shoe. It was spattered with blood. "We think something dragged her into the bushes and ate her," he explained. "It must be some kind of huge beast – probably a big cat or a wild dog."
"How horrible," I shuddered.
"Don't leave camp alone,
and don't hunt at night!"
he warned.

Chapter Three

I ran back to camp and told Tariq, our athletics captain, all about the beast. "If what Eleven said is true," said Tariq, "and a little girl has been taken, then this creature is dangerous."
"I'm surprised Sport Squad warned us," said Ricky, our enormous shot thrower. Even he looked rather nervous. "I thought the Sport Squad would be delighted if we were eaten alive," he joked.

"I think they warned us because they know we're in real danger," said Tariq.
That night Ricky and I were on guard duty. No one in the camp got much sleep.
All night long, we could hear the sound of something crashing around in the bushes, deep in the valley below.
Next morning Ricky said, "It sounded as if there was a whole pack of beasts out there last night."

"It's odd," I replied. "I've never seen tracks for any big beasts on the island. Only tracks for deer and rabbits."
"I didn't know you were an expert tracker," grinned Ricky. "Are you some kind of wildlife expert or something?"

"Not exactly," I smiled. The truth was, I had been watching the animals and birds on the island for some weeks now. Whenever I was sent out to hunt animals, I just couldn't bring myself to kill them. So instead, I had been watching them and learning about them. "I have started to learn about animal tracks," I said.
Ricky looked surprised.
"If you don't believe me, I'll show you," I said. "Come on."
We walked through the valley to where we had heard the crashing noises last night.

"Look!" I said, pointing to the soft mud.
"Footprints!" said Ricky peering over my shoulder.
"This is no beast," I said. "These are human shoe prints. Lots of them. Just like yours or mine."
I pointed to our own tracks leading back towards camp.
"There wasn't any beast here last night," I said. "There were people!"
"Strange," said Ricky, scratching his head.

Chapter Four

Ricky and I followed the tracks. They led towards Sport Squad's camp. Peering through the trees, we saw Sport Squad sitting around a fire. "They are cooking meat," said Ricky. "They must have been hunting." "There's no sign of Rosa," I said, "but look." I pointed to a set of small tracks on the ground to our left. The left footprint was wearing a shoe. The right one was bare.

"Rosa only has one shoe,"
said Ricky. "Eleven showed you
the other one, covered in blood."
"Follow me," I cried, running
alongside the tiny footprints.
"Something very strange is
going on."
The footprints led to a big
hollow tree.
"Listen," I said. We could hear sobs.
"Rosa?" I called. "Are you there?"
I crawled inside the tree. A little
girl was tied up on the ground.
Her big, brown eyes stared
up at me.

"My team left me here all night," she sobbed.

"Why?" I asked, untying her.

"They wanted you to think there was a beast," sobbed Rosa, "so you would stay in your camp at night."

"They wanted to hunt on our land without us catching them!" growled Ricky. "There never was a beast. They made it up to scare us! Cheats!"

"That's why there were so many footprints in the mud," I said, "and they hid poor Rosa in case we saw her and found out that they were lying! They must have covered her shoe with blood from the animals they hunted."

When Rosa had stopped crying, Ricky gave her a piggy-back to the Sport Squad camp.

"You found her," cried their captain, pretending to sound pleased.

"We'll take half your meat as a reward," said Ricky.

"No way!" cried the captain, but Ricky pushed him aside.

"We'll need food for Rosa, too," I said. "She's coming to live at our camp."

"Really?" Rosa grinned. Her big eyes sparkled.

"Of course," I said and held her hand. "We'll keep you safe," I smiled.

"You're on *our* team now."

Quiz

Text detective

- **p4** Find two pieces of evidence that show Lena is missing home.
- **p8** What warning does Eleven bring?
- **p13** Why is Lena suspicious about the story of big beasts on the island?
- **p20** What makes you think Rosa is pleased to live in North Athletic's camp?

Word detective

- **p9** Find a word that means 'thumping'.
- **p15** How does the author let us know that Ricky is puzzled?

What do you think?

What would be worst about being stranded on a remote island? If you were stranded, like Lena, would you make friends with your rivals? Why?

HA! HA!

Q: What do you get hanging from palm trees?

A: Aching arms!

Before reading
A Beast in the Bushes

Characters

- **Tariq** – the North Athletic captain
- **Lena** – a javelin thrower for North Athletic
- **Ricky** – a shot thrower for North Athletic

Setting the scene

Tariq's team has been stranded on a desert island. They have been warned by their rival team that there is a dangerous beast on the island that has killed Rosa, a young hurdler. Now Tariq, Lena and Ricky are on look-out duty.

A Beast in the Bushes

Tariq: Tell me again, what did the boy from Sport Squad show you?

Lena: He showed me Rosa's shoe. It was horrible. It was covered in blood.

Ricky: And Sport Squad think a wild beast ate her?

Lena: Yes. They think it was a big cat or a wild dog.

Ricky: I saw wild dogs on TV, at home.

Lena: Isn't it strange to think about home and TV? They seem like another world.

Tariq: Now we don't even have running water.

Ricky: Or pizza!

Tariq: Trust you to think about food!

Lena: I really want a shower! I want to see if I can find a waterfall on the island, so I can shower in it.

Tariq: No! No one must leave camp while the beast is out there. It could eat you.

Ricky: That beast must be really big if it ate that girl.

Lena: I remember Rosa from the plane. I gave her a sweet.

Ricky: Don't talk about sweets! It makes me even more hungry!

Lena: Rosa looks just like my sister. Poor girl. It's too horrible to think about.

Tariq: I'm scared for us. If this beast …

Ricky: What was that?

Lena: What was what?

Ricky: Shhhh! I thought I heard something.

Tariq: Yes, me too. It sounds like there is something there.

Ricky: It could be the beast!

Tariq: Where is it? It's too dark to see.

Lena: Sounds like it's creeping about over there.

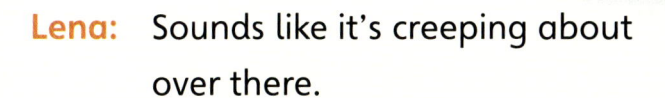

Tariq: We need to scare it away.

Ricky: I could throw this rock into the bushes, where the sound is coming from. That should scare it away!

Tariq: Good idea. You are better at throwing than me.

Ricky: But you're better at running! If the beast appears at least you can run away!

Lena: Don't throw anything for a few minutes. I'll see if I can get closer and see the beast.

Ricky: Don't get too close to it!

Lena: I've got my javelin. If I see the beast, I can throw the javelin at it. That should scare it away.

Tariq: OK. We'll wait here for a few minutes.

(Lena creeps away.)

Ricky: Where is Lena? I can't see her. It's too dark.

Tariq: Listen. I can hear something.

Ricky: I think it's running away!

Tariq: Lena? Are you there?

Lena: I'm here.

Tariq: Are you OK? Did you see the beast?

Lena: I'm OK. It wasn't the beast. It was just a deer.

Tariq: Phew! I thought we were about to get eaten!

Ricky: Talking of eating, I'm hungry!

Lena: Do you ever stop thinking about food?

Ricky: I wish we had pizza to eat.

Tariq: We are on an island. The nearest pizza restaurant is probably 500 miles away!

Ricky: I'm *really* hungry! I can't be on guard all night without eating supper.

Lena: You'll have to – or the beast will eat *us* for supper!

Quiz

Play detective

- p23 What reminds Ricky about home?
- p24 Why are there three dots after Tariq says 'If this beast …'?
- p25 Find a word that means 'moving silently'.
- p25 What evidence is there that Lena is brave?

Before reading
The Beast

Setting the scene

Do you have a cat or know someone who has one? Cats are playful pets but at night they can be fierce hunting creatures!

Poem top tip

As you read the poem for the first time, try to work out what the mystery beast is. Read with emphasis to make it sound mysterious. Then read it with different expression to show the contrast between the happy daytime lines and the fierce night-time lines.

Quiz

Poem detective

- What do you think the poet means when she says the beast 'plays at being tame'?
- What is the rhyme scheme of this poem? What effect do you think it has?
- In verse 4 the poet uses the metaphor 'a silent shadow hunting'. Why is this a powerful image? What does it make you think about?

The Beast

I've seen a beast by Grandad's fire.
Her amber eyes flash bright.
By day she plays at being tame
But her claws come out at night.

I've seen her tangled up in wool
A playful flash of fur.
I've seen her wash her whiskers and
I've heard her gentle purr.

Don't be fooled by whisker washing
Or her gentle, playful purr –
At night she's a prowling shadow
A flash of claws and fur.

I've seen her leave the fire and
Go prowling in the night.
A silent shadow hunting –
Her eyes flash amber bright.

Night shadows leave and day comes in,
The prowling beast is tame.
She's Grandad's gentle, purring cat,
Amber is her name!

by Lou Kuenzler

Before reading

A Famous Castaway

Find out about

- The famous castaway Alexander Selkirk
- How he survived alone on a tiny island
- How he was finally rescued

Tricky words

p31	castaway	**p33**	Pacific Ocean
p32	bullied	**p35**	realised
p32	navigating	**p37**	loneliness

Text starter

A castaway is a person stranded on a desert island. Alexander Selkirk was a castaway. The captain of his ship was angry because Selkirk was better at navigating than he was. Then Selkirk asked the Captain to mend the rotten wood of the ship. This made the Captain so angry that he left Selkirk alone on the island.

A Famous Castaway

A castaway is a person stranded on a desert island. This person is usually a sailor and they usually become a castaway by accident, after a ship hits some rocks and sinks. There are many stories and films about sailors who are stranded on islands by accident.

One of the most famous castaways was left on a desert island on purpose. This sailor's name was Alexander Selkirk.

Alexander Selkirk

In 1704, Alexander Selkirk was on a ship. The Captain was bad-tempered and bullied his sailors. The Captain was terrible at navigating, but Selkirk was very good at it. He used the stars to navigate the ship safely round the dangerous coast of Cape Horn. This just made the Captain even more bad-tempered.

He locked Selkirk in the store cupboard and the other sailors had to set him free.

Next, Selkirk navigated the ship safely to an island in the Pacific Ocean. This island was tiny, but it gave the sailors a chance to drink fresh water and to rest.

A Rotten Ship

One day Selkirk looked closely at the ship's mast. The wood was rotten! Then he found that the bottom of the ship was rotten too. He knew that if they set sail in it, the ship would sink.

Selkirk begged the Captain to chop wood from the island to mend the ship and make it safe. The Captain refused. He ordered the sailors to set sail again in the rotten ship.

Selkirk told the Captain he would not get back on the ship if they did not mend it. He would rather stay on the island alone than die on a sinking ship.

So the Captain left Selkirk on the island. At first, Selkirk thought that the Captain would be back, but as the weeks passed, Selkirk realised that the ship would never come back.

All Alone

Selkirk lived alone on the island for four and a half years. He had many problems on the island.

Food – At first Selkirk just ate lobsters he hunted in the ocean. Then he found goats on the island. He had to hunt the goats on foot and then kill them with his knife.

Rats – Rats were a real problem! They bit Selkirk at night! Then he found some wild kittens. He tamed the kittens and, later, they killed the rats.

Shelter – Selkirk found a cave to shelter in, but bats lived there too. The bats made the cave smelly so later on Selkirk lived in a tent he had made out of goat skin.

Fear – Selkirk heard terrible cries in the night and he thought it was monsters. Later he found out that it was the cries of seals.

Loneliness – Selkirk's worst problem was loneliness. He didn't speak to another human for over four years. He read aloud every day just to hear the sound of a human voice.

Seals

Rescue

After four long, lonely years a ship arrived on the island. The ship's sailors saw Selkirk's ragged beard and goat-skin clothes. They thought he was a wild man. Selkirk told the sailors his story. The sailors told him that the rotten ship had sunk, just as Selkirk knew it would. It hit some rocks and the ship broke up. Most of the sailors on the ship drowned.

If Alexander Selkirk had not been a castaway on the island, he would probably have died on the ship with the other sailors.

Published by Pearson Education Limited, a company incorporated in England and Wales, having its registered office at Edinburgh Gate, Harlow, Essex CM20 2JE.
Registered company number: 872828

www.pearsonschools.co.uk

Pearson is a registered trademark of Pearson plc

Text © Pearson Education Limited 2013

The right of Lou Kuenzler to be identified as the author of this work has been asserted by her in accordance with the Copyright, Designs and Patents Act 1988.

First published 2013

18 17 16 15 14 13
10 9 8 7 6 5 4 3 2 1

British Library Cataloguing in Publication Data is available from the British Library on request.

ISBN: 978 0 435 15256 7

Copyright notice
All rights reserved. No part of this publication may be reproduced in any form or by any means (including photocopying or storing it in any medium by electronic means and whether or not transiently or incidentally to some other use of this publication) without the written permission of the copyright owner, except in accordance with the provisions of the Copyright, Designs and Patents Act 1988 or under the terms of a licence issued by the Copyright Licensing agency, Saffron House, 6–10 Kirby Street, London ECIN 8TS (www.cla.co.uk). Applications for the copyright owner's written permission should be addressed to the publisher.

Designed by Bigtop
Original illustrations © Pearson Education Limited 2013
Illustrated by Nelson Evergreen
Printed and bound in Malaysia (CTP-VVP)
Font © Pearson Education Ltd
Teaching notes by Dee Reid

Acknowledgements
We would like to thank the following schools for their invaluable help in the development and trialling of this course:
Callicroft Primary School, Bristol; Castlehill Primary School, Fife; Elmlea Junior School, Bristol; Lancaster School, Essex; Llanidloes School, Powys; Moulton School, Newmarket; Platt C of E Primary School, Kent; Sherborne Abbey CE VC Primary School, Dorset; Upton Junior School, Poole; Whitmore Park School, Coventry.

The author and publisher would like to thank the following individuals and organisations for permission to reproduce photographs:

Alamy Images / Chris Hellier p35; PRISMA ARCHIVO p38; Getty Images / Jean Baptiste Pillement p31; Imagemore Co. Ltd / pp32–33b; Veer/Corbis / Dereje Belachew p37.

In some instances we have been unable to trace the owners of copyright material, and we would appreciate any information that would enable us to do so.

Quiz

Text detective

- **p34** Why do you think the Captain refused to mend the rotten ship?
- **p36** How did Selkirk overcome each of his problems?
- **p38** Was Selkirk right to refuse to sail on the rotten ship? Why?

Non-fiction features

- **p34** Find three past tense verbs ending in 'ed' in the middle paragraph.
- **p36** How does the layout of this page help you to read and understand Selkirk's problems?

What do you think?

Do you know the story of Robinson Crusoe? That story was based on the life of Alexander Selkirk. How would you survive if you were on a desert island?

HA! HA!

Q: What do you call a baby lobster that won't share its toys?

A: Shellfish!